Brands We Know

Barbie

By Sara Green

Bellwether Media • Minneapolis, MN

Jump into the cockpit and take flight with Pilot books. Your journey will take you on high-energy adventures as you learn about all that is wild, weird, fascinating, and fun!

This edition first published in 2017 by Bellwether Media, Inc.

Library of Congress Cataloging-in-Publication Data

Names: Green, Sara, 1964- author.
Title: Barbie / by Sara Green.
Description: Minneapolis, MN : Bellwether Media, Inc., 2017. | Series: Pilot.
    Brands We Know | Includes bibliographical references and index.
Identifiers: LCCN 2016033337 (print) | LCCN 2016033777 (ebook) | ISBN
    9781626175549 (hardcover : alk. paper) | ISBN 9781681033013 (ebook)
Subjects: LCSH: Barbie dolls--History.
Classification: LCC NK4894.3.B37 G74 2017 (print) | LCC NK4894.3.B37 (ebook)
    | DDC 688.7/221--dc23
LC record available at https://lccn.loc.gov/2016033337

Editor: Christina Leighton   Designer: Josh Brink

Printed in the United States of America, North Mankato, MN.

Table of Contents

What Is Barbie?

It is time for a Barbie pool party! The children dress their Barbie dolls in colorful swimsuits. The dolls go down a slide into the pool. Soon, they are all playing together! After a change of clothes, the Barbie dolls are ready for more fun. One doll soars through space on a hoverboard. Another flies a plane. Barbie can be anything the kids imagine her to be!

Barbie is a fashion doll made by the toy company Mattel, Inc. The company's **headquarters** is in El Segundo, California. In addition to dolls, the Barbie **brand** includes Barbie houses, cars, campers, and other **accessories**. These items add extra fun to play. Barbie movies, books, games, and **apps** are also popular. Barbie is one of Mattel's largest toy lines. People around the world recognize the brand's pink **wordmark**.

hoverboard

By the Numbers

$906 million
in worldwide sales
in 2015

more than
100 people
needed to create a
Barbie doll and her
fashions

$302,500
paid for the
Stefano Canturi
Barbie

150
countries that sell
Barbie products

$3.00
for a Barbie doll
in 1959

more than
180 careers
for Barbie

Mattel Headquarters

The Birth of Barbie

In the early 1950s, Mattel **co-founder** Ruth Handler decided she wanted to create a teenage doll for girls. She knew the idea would be popular after watching her daughter, Barbara, play with paper dolls. Barbara and her friends enjoyed pretending their paper dolls were teenagers or adults with careers. At that time, most toy dolls looked like babies or children.

In 1956, Ruth and her family traveled to Europe. There, she discovered a German doll called Lilli. The doll had blonde hair and an adult shape. After buying the **rights** to Lilli, Mattel hired engineers to make a similar doll. Ruth named this new doll Barbie, after her daughter.

1959 Barbie

In 1959, Barbie **debuted** at the American **International** Toy Fair in New York City. The doll came in blonde or **brunette**, and she wore a black-and-white striped swimsuit. Soon, Mattel began **advertising** Barbie on television. The doll's popularity soared. That year, 300,000 Barbie dolls sold for $3 each!

Barbie's Biography
Barbie's full name is Barbara Millicent Roberts. Her hometown is the imaginary Willows, Wisconsin.

I'll make believe
that I am you
1950s tagline

Elliot Handler

Ruth Handler

New Dolls, Big Changes

The Barbie line quickly grew. Barbie soon had new friends and accessories. The Ken doll, named for Ruth's son, debuted in 1961. Soon after, Barbie had her first house and car. Her best friend, Midge, was introduced in 1963. Skipper, Barbie's younger sister, followed a year later.

Barbie's looks began to change in the 1960s. She had shorter hair and softer makeup. Mattel also began to produce a variety of Barbie dolls. The Twist 'N Turn Barbie debuted in 1967. This Barbie with long, straight hair could twist and bend at the waist. Her outfits came in bright prints. The popular Malibu Barbie debuted in 1971. She came ready to hit the beach with a swimsuit, towel, and sunglasses.

Ken-He's A Doll!
1960s tagline

·········· **1961 Ken**

Malibu Barbie ··········

The variety of Barbie dolls, clothes, and accessories continued to expand through the 1980s. Barbie's clothes changed based on popular **trends**. Professional fashion designers also began creating fancy clothes for the dolls. Barbie dolls with different **ethnicities** came out, too.

Careers and Collections

Barbie is not just a fashion doll. She also helps children explore careers. Since 1959, Barbie has had more than 180 jobs. She started out as a teen fashion model. Later careers included doctor, astronaut, and firefighter. She has even run for President of the United States!

Career Barbie dolls come with clothes and accessories that fit their jobs. Pilot Barbie wears a blue uniform and hat. Eye doctor Barbie wears a lab coat and glasses. She uses an eye chart to check a patient's vision. Several Barbie dolls have served in the armed forces. Their uniforms match those worn by real soldiers.

Each year, Mattel selects a special Career of the Year for Barbie. These have included Mars explorer, film director, and game developer.

Barbie's Career Highlights

1959	Teen Fashion Model
1963	Executive
1965	Astronaut
1973	Surgeon
1985	Veterinarian
1986	Rock Star
1992	Presidential Candidate
1993	Police Officer
1995	Firefighter
1999	Pilot
2000	Olympic Swimmer
2002	Art Teacher
2007	Chef
2008	Soccer Coach
2010	Computer Engineer
2015	Film Director
2016	Game Developer

Veterinarian

Astronaut

Police Officer

Executive

Game Developer

Kids can explore the globe with the Dolls of the World collection. This line was launched in 1980. Newer dolls have traditional clothing, a **passport**, and an accessory. For example, the India Barbie, released in 2012, wears a yellow **sari** and gold bracelets. A small pet monkey clings to her arm. Canada Barbie was introduced in 2013. She wears the wide-brimmed hat, red uniform, and riding boots worn by the Royal Canadian Mounted Police.

A World Record
Bettina Dorfmann owns more than 15,000 different Barbie dolls! She earned the Guinness Book of World Records title for the largest Barbie collection in the world in 2011.

The Siren

Another Barbie collection focuses on famous characters. Superman, Batman, and Wonder Woman are part of this line. Soda Shop Barbie is part of the **Vintage** Look Dolls collection. Many of these dolls are made just for Barbie collectors. They are often more expensive than other Barbie dolls. Collectors may display their dolls for people to admire or keep them safely stored in boxes.

Barbie Moves Forward

Over time, some people have **criticized** Barbie. They believe the doll's thin, unrealistic shape leads girls to develop unhealthy views of their bodies. People have also complained that Barbie dolls lack **diversity**.

In 2015, Mattel responded with new skin tones and hair colors. Then in 2016, Mattel updated its line of Fashionista Barbie dolls. When the line was originally introduced in 2009, it featured dolls with different styles and personalities. Today's Fashionista dolls are still known for their styles. But now they also have features that make them look more realistic. They are available in curvy, **petite**, and tall body shapes. Barbie's original body type is still available, too. The dolls have 7 skin tone options and 22 different eye colors. They also feature a variety of hairstyles and textures. One doll comes with wavy, blue hair.

YOU CAN BE
A DOCTOR

Barbie

THE NEW 2016 FASHIONISTAS' LINE

Imagination comes in all shapes and sizes.

2010s–current tagline

Today, some Barbie dolls and accessories use Wi-Fi and other technology to make play even more exciting. A doll called Hello Barbie understands human speech. She can listen to children and talk back to them in a friendly way about a variety of subjects. Hello Barbie also tells jokes and plays games. In all, she can say more than 8,000 phrases and sentences.

Point of View

When Barbie was introduced in 1959, the gaze of her eyes looked off to the side. In 1971, her eyes were changed to look straight ahead.

You Can Be Anything

2010s–current tagline

Kids can also use technology to create their own Barbie fashions. They use **software** or an app to create and print outfits for Barbie on special fabric sheets. Even Barbie's home uses technology! It connects to Wi-Fi and responds to voice commands. Kids can tell the house to lower the elevator and preheat the oven. The house turns lights on and changes their color. It also has a party option. Lights flash, music plays, and the stairs become a slide.

Barbie's Helping Hand

Over time, Barbie dolls have also helped people. A jewelry designer named Stefano Canturi made a special edition Barbie to raise money for breast cancer research. The doll wore a real diamond necklace and sold for $302,500 in an **auction**.

Mattel also recently created other dolls that were sold to raise money for **charities**. They were part of a new line called Sheroes. Each Shero looks like a female who has made a difference in the world. One is of Sydney Keiser. She is a young fashion designer who started at four years old! In 2016, star ballerina Misty Copeland and Olympic gymnastics champion Gabby Douglas had dolls created in their likeness. Every day, Barbie encourages leadership and imagination!

Gabby Douglas

Dolls That Give Comfort

In 1997, Mattel came out with Barbie's friend Becky, its first doll in a wheelchair. In 2012, the Ella doll was introduced. She had no hair and came with several wigs. Ella dolls were given to hospitals around the United States.

Trisha Yearwood

Emmy Rossum

Eva Chen

Sydney Keiser

Barbie Shero
honorees

19

Barbie Timeline

1959
Barbie is introduced at the American International Toy Fair

1964
Barbie's younger sister, Skipper, joins the family

1971
Malibu Barbie is introduced

1961
Barbie is introduced in Europe

1961
Ken is released

1963
Barbie's friend Midge is released

1965
The first Barbie with bendable legs debuts

1980
The Dolls of the World line comes out

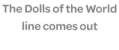

1992
The best-selling Barbie ever, Totally Hair Barbie, is introduced

1999
The Generation Girl series comes out

2009
Fashionistas debut

Misty Copeland Shero Barbie

2015
Sheroes Barbie dolls are introduced

2013
Mars Explorer "Career of the Year" doll is released

1992
Barbie for President debuts

President Barbie in 2000

2015
Barbie introduces a video blog on YouTube

2016
Barbie dolls with curvy, tall, and petite body shapes come out

Glossary

accessories—things added to something else to make it more useful or attractive

advertising—using notices and messages to announce or promote something

apps—small, specialized programs downloaded onto smartphones and other mobile devices

auction—a public sale where goods are sold to whoever offers to pay the most money

brand—a category of products all made by the same company

brunette—dark brown hair

charities—organizations that help others in need

co-founder—a person who started a company with one or more other people

criticized—talked about the problems or faults of someone or something

debuted—was introduced for the first time

diversity—the state of having differences

ethnicities—qualities related to race or origins of a group of people

headquarters—a company's main office

international—coming from outside of the United States

passport—a document that shows someone's citizenship and allows someone to travel to another country

petite—short and thin

rights—the legal ability to use a certain name or product

sari—a long piece of fabric wrapped around the body

software—programs that tell computers what to do

trends—current styles

vintage—something that was made long ago

wordmark—a design of the written name of a company that acts as a symbol

To Learn More

AT THE LIBRARY

Goddu, Krystyna Poray. *Dollmakers and Their Stories: Women Who Changed the World of Play*. New York, N.Y.: Henry Holt, 2004.

Green, Sara. *American Girl*. Minneapolis, Minn.: Bellwether Media, 2017.

Slater, Lee. *Barbie Developer: Ruth Handler*. Minneapolis, Minn.: Checkerboard Library, 2016.

ON THE WEB

Learning more about Barbie is as easy as 1, 2, 3.

1. Go to www.factsurfer.com.

2. Enter "Barbie" into the search box.

3. Click the "Surf" button and you will see a list of related web sites.

With factsurfer.com, finding more information is just a click away.

Index